SPRING MILLS

SPRING MILLS

Poems

MIKE SCHNEIDER

RAGGED SKY PRESS
Princeton, New Jersey

Published by Ragged Sky Press

270 Griggs Drive, Princeton, NJ 08540

www.raggedsky.com

Library of Congress Control Number: 2022950080

ISBN: 978-1-933974-51-4

Cover and book design: Pamela L. Schnitter

Cover photo: EQRoy courtesy of Shutterstock

Printed in the United States of America

First Edition

Contents

*

I was raised in the country, I been workin' in the town
I been in trouble ever since I set my suitcase down
—Bob Dylan

AUGUST NIGHT

Cicada vibrato, sexual
buzz in the sycamores
& thirsty hedges, night
a sizzling wire, high
voltage. A rocking-horse
moon peers out from frazzled
blue cloud & winks like long-gone
Uncle Bob as if to say, Listen.
This is what there is: Furious
commotion. Like bottle
clatter in this garbage tub
I lug to the street. To roar
& want out like words. Waste
is what we throw away
unused. And it comes over me
big & windy as the night
full of crickets, clinking
glass, a mockingbird's
rasp—as if the air
woke from lethargy of being
air, sudden inscrutable
              awareness, tongue
licking up to shape sound
in the mouth of an animal
born to die. I kick the curb
& lean down to pet my old dog
Sam, deaf & blind from cancer,
cells in him blooming untamed
as wind-whipped fire. He plays
his silly game, scratching
              the door to get out,
scratching to come back in
because he wants me
              to give him biscuits.
I give him as many as he wants.

SKIN

Suddenly awake, I shake
         my head & fold my arms
to hold myself. To feel
         myself breathing calms me

like the ocean calms intelligence—
         breath across the tongue, taste
of absence, words not there
         to say when she turned

& touched my arm. Two
         galaxies drawn to the other's
gravity, spiraling round
         each other, stretched & pulled

away from ourselves. I thought
         of sweltering summer, small
town, a boy & his three-legged
         dog named Eddie, how

he wobbled, Eddie, hot cinders
         on the sidewalk by the barber
shop, striped pole like a candy
         cane twirling slowly. Why

did I feel suddenly lonely
         as a stone? *Anything can happen,*
because nothing says it can't.
         She said that. *Let's have a collision*

to obliterate the silence
         of all the words ever spoken. No one
said that. Christ, emptiness,
         nameless, where am I now?

BREATH THROUGH BONES

Gracefully or not, I've arrived
at the age when people get younger
than they were & earnestness
flames beneath the skin
of my daughter's face as she counts time
& waits to lift her silver flute, to form
the embouchure—earnestness that's part of me
at this age when she's the mouth of a long river
flowing into wordless song. Old friends
seem old & my mother can't go out
in the cold. Husbands & wives
are depressed, putting on
weight. The Federal Reserve
says interest is down. Possibility
after possibility, like a mirage
you reach to touch, has disappeared
& slides around shimmering, a word
related to shimmy, the way an Egyptian
dancer moves her hips. My mind
moves like that at this age
& I think I'll be a child who wanders
lost in a dark forest whistling happily
because the cellos are touched with madness—
the slow movement of Beethoven's Seventh.
Listen. Earth is turning, the sound
of breath through bones.

CROWS

Stiletto-tongued, they stab the air.
     Light has come again, they say.
Stir yourself, they insist
    to the farmer. He rubs his eyes.
His grandmother in heaven
         on her kitchen rocker
knows that crows are politicians
    strutting through the House of Lords
in black morning coats with long tails.
    They wear feathers that shimmer
with iridescence as they peck at carrion
    on the highway. Their heads rock
back & forth on spindled legs
    as if knocking at a door. *Knock,*
knock. The farmer hears
        his day's work cry out
to be loved—to mow his field
    where last night a doe
made a bed for her fawn to awaken
    in dew-misted alfalfa. His
cutting machine is business
       of the day. It chews
a ten-foot swath, spits pungent green
    bales without waver, sputter
or cough. Like a crow perched
    high, the farmer peers ahead,
vigilant for sun-glint off an eye, dappled
    brown sack of kicking life, asleep
like an unwritten poem
      to be awakened, brought forth,
awkward, long legs dangled
    from his cradling arms. Already
this year he's lifted three to safety.

*

SPRING MILLS

Memorial Day, 1943

At 17 my father had a silver cornet
& blue light stirred behind his eyes.
He stepped out behind the slide trombones,
march tempo, six abreast, six pair of spats
sparkling white on spit-shine Sunday shoes—
row on row of legs draped in royal blue,
striped with gold, 120 steps a minute
to the rattle of the snare down Main Street.
The music is proud Sousa & my father
swells with breath beneath brass buttons,
mouthpiece pressed to lips, triple-tonguing,
double forte. Bright notes burst into the air
of crystalline afternoon, lilac-scented spring.
    In from the fields on holiday,
a corridor of eyes & smiles, scrubbed
faces framed in white collars, calloused
hands clapping as the band steps by—
These kids sound good, don't they?
    His silver horn sings out *legato*
over Penns Creek where it curves
under the wobbly footbridge by the fire hall.
Stars & stripes ripple from the flagpole
at the Post Office. An old willow leans
over the water, strand after strand of green
tears. A red-winged blackbird screeches,
lifts into the breeze, epaulets flashing scarlet
as it flaps across the creek to the ballfield
like a young man crossing the sea to war.

THE CAR WINDOW

for Melvin "Snip" Snyder

I'm in the back seat of our Ford wagon
or was it the Olds?—with the world
at the hub of the steering wheel, promising
we'll see it all. I'm 12 & it's November,
I think, when early darkness whispers
& I'm inventing incredible love songs
Rebecca of the beckoning eyelids . . .
because Becky Smith wants
to go roller-skating with me. Both
hands on the wheel, my father steers
through the night. At a stoplight, he leans
out to shoot a spout of brown juice
from the Mail Pouch wad in his cheek.
Beside a farmer's field, we pull over.
Nature's outhouse, he says
& my mother says *Snip*, meaning
Please don't. And he laughs
meaning *You don't know.*
A man's life is like this . . .
steam rising as his piss stream
puddles the frosted stubble. Back
on the road, he keeps the window-wing
open, night air like a cold river
rushing into my imaginings
of a hayride, moonlit trees,
Rebecca. I pretend I'm not shivering
with my brothers under olive-drab
wool, scratchy remnant of the Army,
his distant, mythic past. *It's cold,*
says Bobby, who's seven
& doesn't know the drill. The old
man's at the wheel. Pull up the blanket,
shut your mouth. Hold on tight to dreams.

UNTITLED COPPER AND STEEL

a sculpture by Sean Macmillan

Heavy metal creature
                hunkered in the corner
like a fighter as the cutman
              works to stanch the blood

& the bell rings, you
           coulda been more
than a contender, coulda
              been a driveshaft, bent

stovepipe, steel wheel, five-speed
        transmission. Coulda been
a real-deal androgynous
           garage-band desperado.

What a piece of work
        is Stan, I'd say if your name
were Stan, depraved
           as Kowalski, yelping

for your Stella—gone, man,
          gone. You are cold coffee
& leftovers. Raskolnikov
      talking to yourself rudely, wanted

as a criminal in every state
        of anxiety. Scarred & lizard
scaly to the touch, blue
          torch blasted in flares

of spark, you became
          violently yourself. Tiger,
tiger, you've been burned,
        spat on, learned: Beware

of rescuers, strike first, run
      fast. Cruel as a shrapnel burst,
your spread-eagled invitation
        cries out in shameless

joy: Nothing is surplus.
        What fist-like thing
curdled with mother blood
   surges from your flanged opening?

MANAGUA AFTERNOON

On a roof of wrinkled tin
the sun beats a silent drum—
mosquitoes, sweat & restless
dreams. She measures time
in sighs, cries before sleep, wakes
humming a sad radio love-song.
     A few *cordobas* means new
shoes. She's a nurse & lifts
her white shift to show
a half-dollar patch of silvered
skin. *Somocista* bullet, she
says. Barricades of stone
ripped from the street,
crackle of automatic rifle—
a round-headed pellet
of lead spins incorruptibly
through sulfurous air.
The fine hair on her thigh
shines in the sun, lustrous
brown skin gleams.
     Que lastima.
Things we feel & don't
say. Days when endurance
means hold-on dead center,
vacancy at the bottom
of a moment, to be there & see
into the next even more emptied
moment & go on. I refuse
to complete any thought
beyond this bullet-shaped
pellet spinning incorruptibly
through sulfurous air.

NIGHTFALL NEAR MATAGALPA

The fire that cooked our beans & rice
still blazes. Stomach warmed to *café negro*
from a tin cup, I watch flames lick
the darkness. Amanda, one of the cooks,
hums a tune. From the farmhouse, Spanish
sentences crackle & spark. Orchestral
    buzz of crickets, music of night outside
the city anywhere, I tell myself, as the fire
snaps & I slap a mosquito, blood
smeared with sweat across the back
of my hand. From somewhere, a dog barks
at something. Two of the *muchachos*
    crunch the gravel, into the circle
of firelight, their rifles—long spears
of shadow. Boys becoming men
before they're boys, learning to repair
tractors, an unequipped machine shop,
a teacher they revere, Federico, gringo
from Florida, who from nothing—a seed
in his skull, miracles & friends—grew
this school. Pick & shovel six-feet down,
    today we cheerfully dug a trench, roofed
it with two-by-fours, wrinkled tin, a foot
thick layer of sod—enough, with luck,
says Federico, to weather a mortar. Dinner
& after, talk of our murderous fool president
from the actors guild, his evil-empire
nightmare, Federico leading twelve-year-olds
in rifle drill because the *contras* are in these
hills. A quiet man, lanky, with fierce blue
eyes, he nods toward the ridge, a mile across
the valley. From the papaya grove, at a stone
beside the fat sow's mud-patch, each of us
takes a turn. As uncountable stars blink
& crickets chirp & myriad blossoms
scent the air, we watch & listen.

October 1984, The Agro-Mechanization School at El Cacao

WHAT WE'RE PREPARED TO SEE

What's freedom if not to rot
like the carcass of a dog an hour dead
along the highway to Managua?
Sky a swirl of buzzards spiraling
on corridors of air, black-gowned
lords of fresh death, they savor
pungent morning, one-by-one
swoop to earth. Hulked shoulders
strut into the mob, jostle for space
at the feast. What's the body?
The ancient downcurved beak
rips & snatches steaming meat.
        Managua, July 19, 1979, *el pueblo*
the people, triumphant in undulant
waves, swarm the plaza of the National
Palace. They bazooka the proud
equestrian bronze of Somoza
from its pedestal, machine-gun
& hammer it to death beyond
mere lifelessness. They drag the head
through streets. At the left haunch,
half a horse's ass, they empty
their clips, then kick & piss.
        Five years later, half a horse's ass
is what remains, dishonored
in dust, outside the war museum
at the new Eduardo Contreras market
built by the Sandinista government
for *el pueblo*, who wait in jumbled,
indiscernible lines for the bus,
always late & the only payphone,
which doesn't work. Building a new society—
this is not folklore, says my friend, the poet.
We kick the horse's ass, drink Coca-Cola
& see, he says, what we're prepared to see.

WITHOUT MOONS OR LILIES

for Anita

What about murdered poets?
        you asked as you poured cheap
vodka & hoisted a glass to García
    Lorca. To words, you said, that infest
the silken underwear of priests
        & magistrates & make them
itch. Reckless green wind
    clattered the shutters. Lorca

is playing his sky piano, you said,
        because tonight is the Festival
of Wounds that Never Heal. *A world*
    of broken rivers, said Lorca, *in a cat's*
paw crushed by a car. Defeat
    & loneliness swept into the room. Salutes
& boots with spurs, jingle-jangle. To say
    I want & laugh at your voice

saying it, you said & laughed. No stranger
    is stranger than your own heart.
On that white morning at Ainadamar,
    Falange bullets ripped Lorca. Empty
cartridges rattled the limestone
        clapping time to a *siguiriya*
for murdered poets. There were no tears.
    The olive trees, as usual, dripped with dew.

MONOLOGUE FOR LONG AFTERNOONS

for Andy, a Vietnam vet

It's not well known that Freud
was my father, my mother Yogi Berra's
older sister. My mind & body have little
to do with each other. In other words
they get along fine. I dream tall buildings,
44th floor, wind beneath wings. Cigars?—
          I never saw a phallic symbol
I'd smoke. Sometimes I think
     I was killed over there, just haven't
died yet. Ninety-percent of death
is half mental. Yogi didn't say that. I like
blue-collar, hardhat guys, their bigass
machines that gash the Earth & move
dirt. At night, incredible quietness—
the gigantic Cats lie low
                    as cows in a barn. That's
when I leave my bungalow
by the tracks. Under a fat white moon,
I stroll frosted fields to the nursery
of hibernating machinery. I take
my pick. I start one up. It sputters,
roars & away we go, clanking
the speed-bumped streets of suburban
apartment complexes. I become one
with upwardly mobile lovers. I bless
     their stressful professional
dreams. I do this all night till the cock cries
uncle. Then come home to drink vodka straight
from the bottle & dance naked to Jim Morrison's
Hello, I Love You with a Brazilian actress
named Monika who has hips like water
& makes the conga sound like rain.

BEACH BELOW THE HOUSE AT PLYMOUTH

* late afternoon

First there's only the sun, brain
           circuits stunned to blinding
whiteness. Then an intensely yellow
   finch, nearly green with lust, bounces

off three layers of wind. He confettis
        the air with silvery flakes of sound
as if to say, *Look at me. I'm pretty.*
    From the jetty, a fat gull like a wild

trombone squawks operatically
        about being free. What is this surge
& simmer, frothy sentences heaved
   up from deep green distance, unrolling

into the ear of the shoreline? A freighter
    sounds its horn, forlorn. *The sea is huge,*
it says, *filled with sorrow. Do what*
      you must, there's nothing more.

* shadows

From behind & low over my head,
        silken whispered wing-flutter,
tar-black shadow, acid taste of fear—
    Does the undertaker come like this?—

liquidly over white sand, sun-blanched
    driftwood, flotsam of lobster trap, crab
skeleton, yesterday's kelp in blackened
      piles, shadows of the tide marooned

like memory to parch in twisted heaps.
        Aloof pines cast craggy
shadows. They creep toward water. A choir
    of crows scrape the slate sky.

* *morning*

From a farmyard on the bluff,
        a rooster rules the world & commands
Rise up! Already the sun is exploding
    in the east. Stranded on the shoreline,

a green ribbon of seaweed glistens
        crystalline at dawn. On one leg, a gull
occupies his rock. He screams, splitting
        the stillness. Flurry of sandpipers

over sun-flecked water—they careen
    & dip in reckless swerves as if they were
one creature, the wind's inner being
    swooping low & off to wherever it went.

FLOWER MAN

I know a little about a small thing,
      he says, making change
from my Hamilton, handed
    over for a handful of sunny red
& yellow tulips. Will they last
      the weekend? Hell yeah,
he says. You bet. See how
    they're drooped, feelin' pooped?
Cut the ends, put 'em in lukewarm
    water with a few pennies.
They'll stand up straight
      as your pecker. Every night.
You'll see. He grins, chin
      forward, as if he's given me
one of the knowable secrets
    of existence. Alchemy lives,
I'm thinking. Trust me,
      he says. I been with flowers
eight years. He bobs, feints
          a jab. Know plenty
about boxing too. 29 fights.
      Pro. You think I'm a fighter?
Ha. I'm a bricklayer's son,
      he roars. Oh yeah. Exhaust
fume, car horns, walk-light
    flashing. You look pretty good,
I say. Guess you did alright.
      Ha. Brain surgery. I died
twice. He hands me change. Lucky
    to be here. Me too, I say & give
      back two bills. Hey, thanks man.
Sunshine in May, Fifth Avenue, corner
    by St. Paul's. American beauties
for your sweetie, he says. Tulips
    are for kissing. Don't forget your mum.

FLIGHT TO YUCATAN

Happiness is an angel with a grave face.
—Modigliani

Christmas morning, roaring
    south over rumpled hills
of cloud toward Playa del Carmen,
      omelettes & apple pancakes
lofting through the cabin, Zinfandel
      to lift my wings, buoyantly
I'm noticing our flight attendant, waves
    of hair, sable touched with scarlet,
lustrous skin, a pin that says Tamara,
      her smile that says
    you're not the first to look at me.

Wordlessly I wish her happiness
      as down the aisle she brings
the warm container
    of herself. Tamara—
nice name, I tell her, thinking
      of the Goth queen in Shakespeare
who lived only for revenge.

Some people call me Tammy,
    she says with lips glossed persimmon.
We're just having fun here, I say
    to myself & as she turns away want
to untie her apron, want to say
    I'm drowning in your brown eyes, your
dried-blood nails almost make me cry.

Beside me, flipping
      shiny pages
of an airline magazine, my wife
      lifts her eyes—umm, tasty
she says, taking a small bite
      of her apple pancake

with syrup. She smiles
with icy sweetness, woman
I love, my life. Out the window,

stratospheric blue, thin skin
of the planet, clouds
miles below, endless as belief
              & failed promises, vapor
that doesn't catch us when we fall
                through sky that shimmers
like a gift: July for Christmas. A face

is such a strange thing. Obsessed
             with distortion, Modigliani
loved elongated faces
            like Tamara's at a distance,
a flattened oval, two black jewels. He
    painted with a dagger
in his teeth, they say, to see the face
          within the face—grave,
cold-eyed as Nefertiti, Queen of Egypt,
        whom I've always loved
             for her name alone.

RAINY NOVEMBER AGAIN

Morning after the breakup, taste
of last night's coffee, love—
the mixmaster blender, grinder
setting—how it splatters
            you like cranberries
bleeding down the kitchen wall
cause I forgot to hold the lid on
tight. It was Thanksgiving in Houston,
        the year the hurricane
ripped through my brother's suburb
howling like some wounded animal
they haven't named yet. Days
that disappeared in shattered glass
from tall buildings. Lifetimes
            you spend to get it right
& never do. Chrysanthemums
for Nancy, my neighbor, thanks
for taking in my mail & her husband
                wants to stone me.
No good deed goes unpunished
says Jeffers, who likes to say things
        like that. Everything is change,
says Myles, who reads the Dalai Lama
& paints in late light, landscapes
like contusions with a purpled inner glow.

HOW WELL I GO WITH SAND & GRAVEL

for Charley

Hill? Hell, this is rock face
                risen like damnation
from the core. I've crammed my feet,
   chiseled with my fingers
for a grip, braced against the shift
        of stone. Listen to the clatter
as it crumbles, faithless gravel—
            I hear it rattling in my sleep.

I've hugged boulders closer
    than I've hugged my mother, rubbed
my belly sore on limestone, stretched
       to make the final handhold, a root
caked with clay, twisted like an arm
          reaching out from underneath
the cliff-edge. Take hold now—
        it beckons. Pull harder.

Days & days I've clambered,
         come back down, sniffed
the fragrance of myself, learned
        how well I go with red clay,
sand & gravel. It's then I've found
   my mind unwrinkling like a grin
across a child's face, round as the moon,
        one enormous eye, opened wide
to every particle of star-splattered space.

*

SPRING MILLS FOR CHRISTMAS

In from the cold
        to that warm room,
we greet the tree,
        immense with silence—
drape its green branches
        with silver hair, globes
of delicate glass like cherries
        perfectly ripened, too beautiful
to pick, lambent necklaces of light.

We buckle floppy boots & tumble
        out the door with cousins
& Albert the neighbor, trudge
            past the smokehouse
uphill to the edge of the mountain,
        where plush white blankets
unroll from the shadowy woods.

We pack ourselves on board.
        Uncle Ralph gives a running
push & our Lightning Glider
                churns the icy whiteness,
particles of light like pixies
        whirled up from the Earth
to pelt our eyes with magical
        frozen dust that melts
on our faces, stinging us alive,
        christened in tears & laughter.

We were certain of ourselves,
            voices that rang like bells
through the cold as darkness fell,
        noses dripping, wide eyes
            blinking like stars.

FASTBALL SHY

Hot roller to the shortstop,
me—lean machine
of summer, scuffling
in ballfield yellow dirt.
Off like a hound I go
with my three-finger
Warren Spahn, neat's-foot-
oiled cowhide glove
to gobble that scorched
grounder & fire it
across the diamond
to Tub McMullin's
fat-handed mitt at First.
Little League? Shit.
This is ultimate Big Time.

    Who knew that stitched
leather ball could baffle
hand & eye with wild
chance? Wicked hop,
they said, nasty chop
direct to the cartilaged
bulge of my Adam's Apple
dropped me flat, washed
me in starlight. Nerve
& muscle inscribed
with solid-state physics,
I learned to flinch & never
could unlearn that secret.
One rainy afternoon
on Heckman's front porch
we unraveled it, yards
& yards of yarn down
to the inscrutable rubber
pill, unforgiving hard
center of the world.

THE LICKING

Drop your underwear, he says
and lean across that chair.
He loosens from his slacks
the leather strap. Down
it slaps, a losing hand
of cards laid flat, read 'em
& weep. *Keep count,*
he says. Two, three, slash
marks on a chalkboard,
black, no eraser. Four, five—
they sting, a hive of hornets.
The trick: be cold inside, hold on
tight as Sunday shoes, numb
as a thumb in cool blue
jelly, the plum of his eye.
Six. Soon I'll be fixed,
grow up like him & shoot
with a real gun. Lucky seven
rhymes with heaven. Eight
unlocks the gate, cracks the—
damn I'm sobbing, a wretch.
This hurts me more than you,
he croaks, choked up & wet.
Yes boss. I love you too.
Teach me the laws to live by.
Get a good job. Cash the check.
Pay taxes. There is no Santa Claus.
Say goodnight, some quiet mending,
happily-ever-afters never ending.

JUST IN CASE

Is this really happening?
he asks, hands flat on the table,
     fingers skimming the grain
of old wood, texture
     of an oak tree's fat
    & lean seasons, icy nights,
first shoots of winter wheat,
    August, fields of green corn
       whistling at the moon
in wide valleys that lie
     between the stone ridges
where he tramped & hunted.

Words that gurgle as they well up—
     flappy flesh-hole in the throat
slashed from inside, lower-earth rumble
   of the windpipe sucking air.
The squamous cell is vicious,
       a virulent carcinoma,
said the doctor, knowing
     the man wants no evasions.

Yes, it's really happening.
  His hand slides to grip my wrist.
Out the window, robins flutter
       in the dogwood.

Underneath the cushion
of the recliner where he leans back
& tries to sleep—to be horizontal
is to drown in seepage—
   I found his snubnose .38
       fully loaded.
In the valley farms, they spread manure—
  ah, the sweetness. Silos full

with chop, Guernseys
in the pasture, feeding time
they bellow.

Just in case, he says—
looking at me square across the table,
ancient eyes, desiccated yellow face,
50 years, circumscribed by eight hours
a day times five, equals
your life, to provide,
sacred obligation, coded in the genes.
Sacred: change two letters you get *scared*—
what you feel when death stalks
the room where you sit
watching robins flutter in the dogwood.

COUNTRY OF SILENCE

Match your playing to my passion
while I mark the air with time
says the conductor's baton

& your hand moves like that
between us, bringing words
to silence, as if love

could cross a mountain pass
into another country where we speak
in music & you, a cello,

tremolo into a wave that wants
to break, but doesn't
except into the next silence

which roars like the almost vacuum
of space without stars or galaxies,
& I'm the echo of that, a train

at three a.m. howling in A-flat
as if to say the two-year heifer
in the back pasture, white-foamed

mouth spilling a tongue, in birthing
her calf has suffered more than we can
bear, so that when the farmer's son

with a .45, three lead slugs,
opens a crater above the brow
of her skull & she cries out

in agony, heaves up & falls
back into the silence we came from,
we are filled with sorrow & glad.

THE PAINTER FRANCIS BACON
PLAYS MOUNTAIN MUSIC

He scratches on the gut strings
        of a fiddle, ancient tune,
winter wind
   like knives across a hilltop.
A lone oak strains upward
        imploring the dull sky
with long fingers, black
        etched on gray.
Oh, the dreadful wind and rain.
He draws it from his skull, tune
     like the frozen skin of a river,
barbaric ice, silence
        stabbed by a crow's call,
   shadow that floats on the ice.
She pushed her sister in the river to drown.
Watched as the rushing water pulled her down.
He plays the old way, refusing to sing
        with his bow—screeches
as if the tune were marked:
   Play like a scar
        down the side of a face.
The face—bulging red earlobe, nostril
   distended, boar's tusk for a nose,
        black hair sprouting like rope.
A scar that won't heal,
        as if there aren't words
   or no one can speak them,
as if the tune said: Play as if beauty
        is ugliness & ugliness is beauty
   with the skin peeled away.
And the only tune that fiddle could play
        was oh, the wind and rain.
Oh, the dreadful wind and rain.

ROOSTER

Witching hour, three a.m., my father
stirs me from sleep with his campfire
guitar, as if we're in the kitchen, dishes
wiped & stacked, when from the closet
he'd haul out that pawnshop Sears
six-stringer, its barracks repertoire
of Ragtime Cowboys, Darktown
Strutters. He'd strum & vocalize
till bedtime. Then before the sun
he'd rise, sit with a mug of thick coffee
in silence, pack wax-papered
sandwiches he'd carefully wrapped
the night before into his lunchbox—
black, a broken handle he'd fixed
with pliers & wire. He'd lift it, cross
Centre Hall Mountain, 14 years
walking the cell blocks, Rockview
State Pen. Real place, locked
doors, sullen men. He watched them
till the cells of his throat broke
from their regulated life into the unrepentant
paroxysm of freedom that choked
& claimed him long before he showed me
how to write this poem. The dead
stay with us in dream.
    Awakened, I sit here getting a grip.
The woman he loved, my mother, alone
in the stone house where he withered.
What lessons of heart & nerve
must I learn to play that painted cowboy
guitar, to pick the bass notes with my thumb
like a man who speaks no empty words
& sings the old songs? He opens
his throat to crow like a golden rooster
when the sky is pink & yellow & green.

PHOTOGRAPH IN *TIME*, 1985

War is peace. Freedom is slavery. Ignorance is strength.
—George Orwell, *1984*

A man in battle camouflage holds a machete
at the throat of a peasant farmer on his knees
genuflecting in a shallow grave he just dug.
Far from the scene of this photo
our free-world leader speaks.
Into a microphone, he says
of the men in camouflage
that they are "freedom fighters,
the moral equivalent of a founding father."
The farmer's terrorized eyes
gaze from the page of the magazine,
which doesn't show the blade
cutting the stem where life flows
to a living brain, heart's rhythm
visible in spouting blood, lungs'
rasp & gurgle, last gulp of air. Killing
face-to-face is grotesque business.
The moral equivalent of a founding father
does it with practiced, awful grace.

　　　*

Dawn, a quiet highland valley,
low clouds drift with smoke from cooking fires,
scent of corn tortillas—
freedom fighters
sift toward sleepy San Gregorio,
a few tin-roof shelters, families
scratching stony bean plots
to survive, resettled
from the northern war zone
by their government,
"a cruel clique of Godless men,"
says our leader, the great communicator

who paints his words on waves of air
that flow to the people as he speaks
about people he refuses to meet or talk with.

With assault rifles and grenades
the freedom fighters set their ambush
by the hut that serves as school.
The great communicator doesn't say this.
And our newspapers don't tell us.
And memory hungers not to forget
thunder of Hotchkiss guns in South Dakota,
shrapnel tearing infant flesh, a photo—
the old chief hooded in a white rag,
his frozen corpse rising from the snow.

Now there are six children
aged five through eleven,
life evacuated from twelve brown eyes.
And their teacher, a pretty young woman
from Managua, whose father, a man
of private enterprise, friendly to our leader,
says, sadly shaking his head, he doesn't know
what she was doing there anyway.

　　　　*

Sunday in September—
freedom fighters launch their rocket
toward a bus, northbound, the road to Jinotega.
Flame of gasoline explosion—
black smoke with a red tongue
licks & whispers into the air
that freedom is not just a word—
19 women, traveling to visit their sons,
in the Sandinista army
near Matagalpa, are dead.

The freedom fighters dissolve
into cloud-forest mountains
of wild green parakeet, squirrel monkey & jaguar
where they don't hear our leader talking & talking,
where they know killing face-to-face is grotesque business.
We watch the face of business as it smiles,
talks about God & freedom
& says "moral equivalent of a founding father"
with practiced, awful grace.

WESTERN MEDICINE

March 2003, bombs over Baghdad

Talking faces on TV assure me
    that our air strikes on Baghdad are precise
& surgical. My dentist Thelma
               dons her mask & leans
into my mouth. Innocents, say sober
      talking heads, are not the target. I think

of my daughter, fair-skinned,
    blonde. I feel the pinch, precisely sharpened
steel entering my gums as Thelma
           numbs me. Into the mouth of Baghdad
stealthy bombers swarm like blackbirds.
        I hear Thelma's howling drill.

Relax, I tell myself & fold my hands.
        I wish this were over. Our missiles
strike like matches flashing into flame.
        The blue-eyed commander, jaw
settled on destruction, says *Good*
    against Evil. Thelma reaches for her scraping

tool. After you say the words, *Good*,
        Evil, where do they go? Do they rise
in the smoke from charred bones?
          Is it lucky to die? They don't
ask that on TV. Above her mask
    Thelma's trained eyes peer into my mouth.

Eyes closed, I think of flat blue sea,
         slate sky. I want this to be over.
A woman on TV, polished teeth, glossy
    lips moving say—*Surgical. Precise.* Words
like anesthetizing vapor drift & dissipate
        in soft pillows of cloud while worlds

away, a busy marketplace in Baghdad,
          a young woman, dark eyes, jet
black hair, inspects an avocado.
              She's not my daughter. Thelma
drops her mask, smiles, says *We're done.*
          I spit blood & rinse.

SALEM HILL HYMN SING

The Angel of Death is abroad in the land,
only you can't always hear the flutter of its wings.
—Winston Churchill, 1945

A screaming comes across the sky
like a low-flying jumbo. Crescendo.
Decrescendo. Same old thunder.
I can't remember why, but the old books
clamor for revenge. And the congregation
sings *What a Friend We Have in Jesus*—
no wisecracks, not a derisive twitch
in the room. I think of Gaylord Heckman
across the street from my cousin Danny's
with a hand-drill, digging out the center
of a sawed-off broomstick, tacked on
tobacco-tin fins, black powder packed
    in to make a rocket. Keith
is telling me about his beloved uncle
who died & they jimmied the lid on his attic
trunk. Not even his wife knew he was grand
wizard of the local Klan, white sheets, pointy
hoods carefully folded. Now they're singing
On a Hill Far Away, The Old Rugged Cross
    & in the kitchen with a beer, Tom
brays about that time he beat the holy crap
out of some queer. Half-crazy, redneck
Tom who everybody laughs with & loves
because, well, he's Tom. The cops told him
Yeah man, we know where you're comin'
from but there's laws now to protect
those people. Then Lorraine, brave heart
chiming like a temple bell: For two men
to exchange vows, she says calmly, is sanctified
union. She turns & walks away & all the way
home Tom's behind us on his Harley
        in a white hood, flaming cross

on his handlebars like a branding iron. God's
truth screaming in the night, crescendo,

           like a low-flying jumbo, down
Cresson mountain, where neon white light
beams ridge-to-ridge that JESUS LIVES.
    And I'm trying to explain to everyone
not listening, not even in the room anymore,
that those crossed spars on a hilltop far away
from this distance at sunset give a mythic red
glow of suffering that we love too much. Or
not enough. Or is it—casual tolerance
of intolerance—simply fear? The Old
God holy books clamor for revenge & do not
save us from anything. Still, I love that raggedy
piano & to hear them sing, *Come to the Church
in the Wildwood, Little Brown Church in the Vale.*

HOUND DOG BLUES

People all over the planet, millions of them,
are considerably more dead than I am,

I keep telling myself. And this woman
who fell asleep on my couch while I played

You Ain't Goin' Nowhere & other lonesome
songs on my best guitar is not to blame. Please,

she said, play, so I did. And my confidence,
already worn to a thin pale stone, is now lost

& hiding in the dark with hairy animals
who live underground & huddle close

at 55 degrees Fahrenheit, temperature of bones
in coffins. And it came up somehow, before

tired & becalmed she drifted, how Ginsberg
one afternoon, content after masturbating,

heard the voice of Blake & it sank within
to become his own prophetic rumble

from the Earth, like stones if they could speak
with rhythm & radiance. Like the rattling

I heard moments ago—a necklace
her daughter made, small stones scattered

on my hardwood floor. How right it is
to be on my knees gathering these pebbles

into my hand while my refrigerator
purrs like a cat to make things cold.

I WANT YOU

in your pink underwear
        that makes me think
               of jelly beans, want you

as if you were an inscrutable
        message within me. Want to chew

& swallow mouthfuls
    of you. And still want you, Monday
        Tuesday in the old garage

where it's cool & smells like grease
       & my father's tools on the wall

are there to be used like I want
      you to use me, to wear each other

through like work shirts worn
     past threadbare. My hand, how it wants
      to be a sail that can lift

& make you fly, as if you were milkweed
      that bursts into seeds
           lighting the blackness

around us. And the aftersmell—
     morning fog, sweetfern
         flaked with pepper.

LOVE ME LIKE THE FIRST WORD

hello, that rises from loneliness
& what the hell & artificial
flowers in cheap hotels become fragrant
& fragile & you know it won't last

but the country radio plays
slide ukulele blues & the DJ
says Maui & a wave
lifts us with long green fingers

until there's a pool
of underwear & you love me
generously as Brahms, that B-flat
murmur of the cello opening
the window to blue-blazed April

sky of the mind & we forget
all warning of storm, caught
in our experiment like amoebas
in a drop of pondwater
& a biologist somewhere

watching says Holy Shit
as boundaries dissolve & I become
a tadpole, sprout legs, climb
onto a lily pad, croak

to the Rose Moon of summer, round
& white enough to swallow me
as the egg swallows one anointed
sperm & the rest, millions of them,

die trying, while cellphones ring
all over the planet & spy satellites
fall from orbit & olive trees in Madagascar
blanch at our beautiful shamelessness

as you love me like poverty
the mother of crime, death
the mother of beauty, Zappa
the mother of invention

until I'm motherless
as Seth on Craig Street
with his plastic cup into which my quarter
drops with a clink & he says God
Bless & I feel lucky to have breath
& change in my pocket

as you love me majestically spread-winged
as a condor on a thermal updraft in the Andes—
that easy, floating, to stay right there

until I cry
& every word
means tenderness, every gesture
kindness & I forgive my parents
& even the rattle of the air conditioner is joyful noise
like old bones getting ready to dance

ACROSS THE DISTANCE THAT NIGHT

for Lorraine

the way your fingers
curl around the belly
of a cello, carved maple
burnished to glow, almost alive
as you lift & place it
like precious pearl into the shell
of its case, because music
has ended & the spine
loosens as nerves gather waves
from the air, after-music
wakened in the hollow of bones

the way words of a poem
wait their turn, shuffling down corridors
until you least expect a door
to open, mouth to move
& say Leaves of the sweetgum tree
are yellow stars
fallen into your hand, as if the sky
could shatter in small pieces, each
torn fragment pungent
as bread in the morning, when you & I
are gloriously alone, time
having strangely failed
to move us, blanket rumpled, sheet
twisted between us

the way your hand like a boat
on dark water rowed
across the distance that night
you touched my wrist, the way
the sun lifts from blackness
to slant through the blinds
& brighten your hair
on the pillow beside me. Everything
is here, right here.

SLEEPLESSNESS

goes round & round the empty
space in my skull like skittery small
creatures. They scurry

in run-on sentences
made of hungry verbs. Their tiny jaws gnaw
each granule of time, only to find

vacancy, no way
to fall through the hayhole in the windy barn
of sleep. Across the hall

a five-year-old cries out
from his dream of monsters. His mother, beside me
sighs. Like a millwheel

slowly pulverizing, stone
on stone, thoughts to powder, night swallows
day. From the mossy

bottom of a well, a voice
burbles up to say *I am a heliotrope.* Firmly,
as if I should know this

about myself. Sleep, a black
limousine, waits to enfold me while sleeplessness
jangles its old-time gangster

jazz—alert, cold desire. Inside
the long sedan's tinted windows, I see faces, sly
smiles as they joke about sin

that keeps us awake. Grace,
grace, who hasn't fallen from grace? says the whole
high-school cheerleading squad.

Ready or not, here I come, says tomorrow.

*

ICE CREAM

How could I have been prepared
for this?—little-boy face, fat cheeks
squinched to the eyeballs, salty
water seeping up to become
Biblical deluge, agonized weeping

because he finished his ice-cream
cone (double-fudge chokha-mokha)
& wanted a lick of mine
(killa-vanilla with sprinkles).
We were playing a game, making
up names for flavors. *Please,*
he said so sweetly. *OK,*
I said, *you can have some*
(his eyes gleamed). *But first*
  say the magic words—

SPARKLED FIREFLY SQUISH

My four-year-old buddy, as much
as he wanted, couldn't make
his brain, mouth, tongue produce
this jambalaya of sound—

his face, silly putty, spontaneous
meltdown, anguish for a moment
inconsolable. *I'm so sorry,*
I said as I drew him close enough
to quiet the sobs & gurgles surging
up from some unfathomed
bottom of the ravenous sea
where we scream for ice cream.

So sorry, I said, but how could I
not love that little-boy face,
the moment within the moment

before it crumples like a cake
gone flat & hopeless?—how it holds
for an eyelash flicker, strains
          not to let go. Then goes.

OLD BLUE VOLVO

Twenty horses and a crank starter—
　　never made 'em better
　　　　than the Tin Lizzie
said Grandpa, a machinist
　　　　　　at the brass mill,
the Model T a shining image,
　　　　　　youth & freedom.
Henry Ford—two words jangling
　　in his pocket: Living wage.
　　　　Eight-hour day.

Dad loved the '48 half-ton
　　　　he found for a few bucks,
gave it fresh plugs, a bumper, played
　　with the timing till it hummed.
Loved me too,
　　though he couldn't say it.
With that rattly pickup showed me
　　　　manual transmission,
　　　　　　hands-on, sequenced
pattern of the letter H, metallic
　　　　industrial click
of shifting gears. Quietly
　　　　he'd shake his head
as that old truck bucked
　　& quivered to a dead stop.
Feel the free play in the pedal.
　　Let it out slow, then give it gas.

Soon, I was double-clutching
　　　　on the downshift,
drawing raw joy
　　　　from the engine's roar
& surge, pulling deep
　　　　into the furnace of itself
to charge uphill

like a young man
propelling himself into the world.

Now it's my daughter, sixteen,
                         at the wheel.
Our old blue Volvo jumps.
    The dashboard lights up red.
She groans. Quietly
            I shake my head—
this strange voice
          on my tongue.
Let it up till it grabs, then feather it.
      Easy. That's the way.

GUAYABA

Tropical afternoons like a long boat
with black sails & a sharp prow
splitting the air, thick with emptiness
& anguish, drizzle of foreign tongues,
words & meanings like stray stones
in the street, skipping away—
      I remember orange flowers
like early stars bristling at twilight,
the distant tree of fire
arbol de fuego & there
in the flickering light of memory—
   slender ankle
undisturbed through the dust
she came like a small deer, young girl
bringing this strange hard fruit, *guayaba*.

I took it, biting hard, as she showed me
the fruit yielding, *dulce* she said,
soft & pink, *rosita* she said,
the color of dying light.
   Quietly as sunset, wholly
as indifferent to me or anything
      she turned toward the mountain.

I felt the certainty & grace of evening
approaching shadow by shadow,
the print of her cotton skirt
sinking into a remnant of memory,
   woodcut on a thumbed page.
I saw a jaguar flitting across a road,
slipping into a field of corn
so quickly I wasn't sure I'd seen at all.

Soon there was a white moon.
      It was October & cool.
There were her brown eyes

      & a smile, not even a smile,
gesture without gesture—
     an arm lowered to reveal
thin wrist, fingers opening, palm
            full of sweet green *guayaba*.

          Esteli, Nicaragua, 1984

YA NO PUEDE

A scuttling sound like plaster crumbling
from the lath that lines the walls—
The rats again, but don't screw in the bulb.
Burnt out, and who can afford the black market?
says Conejo, the rabbit, head of the household
where I lie awake, head drumming
with last night's talk, tongues silvery
with La Plata, cheap white rum
we sip from coffee mugs. *The traffic*
goes one way, he says, *and it's not my way.*
Lumber, 200 cordobas a board!
The caged green parakeet, *parajito,*
half bald, squeaks a sickly chirp.
Three years ago it was five. I'm a carpenter.
Ya no puede, he says, eyes blazed to black,
laughing madly—*I can't do it.*

                    *

Damn that crazy rooster in the courtyard.
El gallo loco. Might as well be scraping
on my ear the way he crows each
morning, before the halo of first light.
Sunday dinner, Mauricio calls him.
From gawky fledglings he raises
roosters, pushes them at each other
in afternoon heat, goads them
till they kick & peck & their spurs
draw blood that spatters the dust.
If he runs he's no fighter. I wring
his neck & boil him. Sunday dinner.

                    *

In the kitchen, Gloria nurses a small fire
to save wood—warm scent of smoke,
fresh tortillas she rolled yesterday.
The parasites, says Conejo, *eat her from inside.*

Mother of my children. We have new clinics
with no medicine. What can I do? Life
is hell. Cathedral bells ring
& ring again. Six a.m. mass.
A sad-eyed dog shuffles to the doorway
begging food. Gloria snaps her fingers.
He slinks away, a well-trained stray.
How many kicks in the ribs does it take?

    *

Still, the morning is beautiful.
Elotes, elotes, ears of sweet corn
in a basket on her head, a woman
calls from the street. *Oh, father in heaven*
hear my prayer. Conejo kneels
at his cot in the small room we share.
This day bless and protect my family.
He mutters into his beads. *A few weeks*
and you fly away, he says. *We'll still be here.*
I lift myself & stumble to the tin stall
in the courtyard, where a trickle of cold water
splashes my back as I look up
at the wakening sky, still rosy & blue
in streaks, and gray, sprinkled with faint stars.

              Esteli, Nicaragua, September 1984

DARK MATTER

The souls moving along . . . . are they invisible
while the least atom of the stones is visible?
                    —Walt Whitman, "Song of Myself"

It's fizzy out there in the universe
& the physicists are looking for you,
dark matter. You hide, but they know
you're there, in their gray matter
        see you glittering, slippery
as thought, how it slides away
            like What's her name?—
that violin player I used to know. Evenings
in her garden, springtime fragrance
of turned earth —how happy she was.
Poof. Vanished to the Smoky Mountains
where, dark matter, you surely flourish.

                    *

Because you hold the galaxies
in place, I hear myself rumble,
lightning in the neurons, word sounds
        on the tongue—How could
I not remember?—Roberta.
Her favorite key, A minor,
sorrow—how she'd set it free
in waves. Dear mother, dark matter,
        without you I'd be unglued.

                    *

Sometimes in my inner ear
        I hear you mumble: *Turn*
            around. Curtains
flutter, face at a window, lonely
old man across the street. His ghostly
            white Siberian husky, evil-eyed,
howling at the round moon, wavering

heart-cries of anger & longing.
It must have something to do with me
        & you, dark matter, though
I don't know why I turned
        or if I heard anything at all.

      *

Illusory, everywhere
        at once, like the sea
in which my fingers as they move
to make sentences are a net
        to catch the sound of someone
in there scratching to get out—
        hieroglyphs, strokes of ink
on sheets of pulp & rag—
        dark matter, you inhabit space
& time & are with me
        when I wake at the darkest hour
as if dropped here from another world
    asking, *What wild kingdom is this?*

ONCE UPON A TIME

Think of it this way: Somewhere
a twitchy trigger-finger, speck
of ferocious energy freed, kernel
of a seed still sprouting, source
of every impulse to move,
    says the physicist in love,
the cosmos of himself unfolding
like a rose in bloom.
    This attraction, me to you,
he says, biochemical vibration, voodoo
at the fingertips, is that same blossoming.
A quantum glitch, leakage from some
wormhole, like the first firefly
of summer, birth without conception
bursting from whatever darkness
there was when there was only
absence, into the light of everything
that's happened—immeasurable
violence, he says, hapless
    passenger on the freight train
of his chromosomes, electrons
hopping broken rails of nerve.
We're bumper cars, he says, careening
through a curve in space-time, strange
quarks, immortal protons, twisted
strands of DNA. What a ride
to arrive here, two lonely helices,
one enchanted evening, fingers
gliding up & down the neck
of a guitar. Django Reinhardt
was made of stardust, chains
    & rings of carbon. Let's
tango, let's twist a little closer, let's
misbehave, he says, like an organic
chemist who knows a few old
tunes. Eros loosed the arrow, time

flying all directions, no direction
home, he says, like a lawyer
of thermodynamics. Love
is evolution of the cosmos.
What else can we do?
    he says, becalmed at last—
as if talking on his grandmother's
front porch, beside her on the glider.
Summer evening quietness. A breeze.
The big tree across the street.
Everything made sense.

ODE TO LONELY GUYS

i.m. Leonard "Doc" Frank

lonely as one petunia in a flowerpot
lonely as the letter z
    waiting for the next letter
lonely as the first word spoken
lonely as an empty tank of gas
    two a.m., a back road in Alabama
lonely as the day the payment's due
    midnight, knock at the door
    South Street, among the crack deals
    & half-dead drunks
lonely as a hound in heat,
    Willy Loman out of town
    making time with lonely women at a bar
lonely as a hundred dollars from my mother
    who says *Do something nice for yourself*
    To give it to Tailisha at The Cricket
    Lounge felt good & still
I'm lonely as a broken string on my guitar
    shaped like a woman that my fingers
    strum to make her sing, lowdown
    & blue as Judas, the morning after,
    last night's wine turned to urine
    as doubt creeps in. *Conscience*
    is only weakness of the brain,
    says Rimbaud & I'm still
lonely as an equation, love times the speed of light
    equals empty space, a blank page, freedom to be
lonely as the watchman at the mushroom factory
    just before dawn, when he tastes the air
    & hears the mushrooms groan.

HOW MANY FACES DO YOU HAVE?

I like to be touched, says Alicia, words
splashing against me like rain on tulips.
Spring thirst & the early bird catches

words fresh from her mouth. *The art
of living,* she says, *means take the gift
of yourself seriously.* It's good to hold

you, I say to her skin that holds sunlight
& warms me until we're empty & sleep
fills us & we don't exist. Love arrives

in shiny raindrops, she dreams, each of us,
as if thought by Magritte, holding an
unremarkable black umbrella. The hotel

bellman, his face, wrinkled bronze beneath
the brim of a brown bowler, crimson
jacket, buttons polished gold. *What do you like*

most about yourself? he asks, eyes that burn
acetylene blue. Each moment bleeds into the next
soldier home from war, beribboned, handsome

with sadness. Is this my father? Poems
like money hidden in shoes, many shoes
in the room. Alicia's not here. The bellman,

his eyes—how can I answer? *I treat people
well,* he says & turns away. I drop tender green
in his brass spittoon, open-mouthed, a rictus,

a scream. *I like to be touched*, says Alicia.
To be free as a river means want nothing
outside yourself. The art of living—

sun-sparkled dew on tulips. *How*
many faces do you have? In a startling
moment, a woman once asked me this, eyes

deadbolted with mine. She flashed ten of her
most beautiful & terrifying faces. Seconds
passed. Then she asked, *How many more?*

BUENOS AIRES

I'm not the *I love you* that closes a phone call
as if filling out a form, she says. I'm the kiss

that says OK, here's a wet one for you on the lips—
now leave me alone because it's the frayed end

of the day & your breath of nerves & steel
coffee reminds me of how tired I am, to see

you come through my door in that well
meaning, innocuous way, when what I want

is to be chopped & sizzled, defenses obliterated
like Vesuvius obliterated the merchants

& whores, mothers & lovers of Pompeii—
all in a day's work. Like kitchen roaches

in nuclear winter, you & I survive. We
go on. The inane Q & A proceeds. Please

give me a toothache. A new appliance. A layer
of fresh snow. A minute to compose myself.

This flash fire stoked by low wind downslope
from the mountain has withered to embers

& you keep trying to be some kind of poem
about daffodils while the sky roars with dandelion

laughter, thousands of tiny parachutes in slow
descent beginning to begin all over again.

THE TROUBLE WITH LOVE

The trouble with love,
                says a friend of mine,
is you give it an inch
                it takes you dancing,
takes you to lunch
        & the cleaners, takes you
where your mother said
                Don't go. And your father
went & came home
                begging forgiveness.

The trouble with love
                is ice cracks, Earth
howls when love arrives
                like a crocus in spring
if it could cry with joy
                as it heaves toward light.
Open the windows. Love
        is the best drug there is.

The trouble with love
                is hit the road Jack.
You're an empty sack.
                        To be alive is to lose
the world like Bonaparte,
        alone on that high shelf
of the fire escape
                where you look down
at your feet. And think

the trouble with love
        is a wild white flag, deer
in a distant snowfield,
                flashing, gone, bloodhound

sniffing a scorched trail
                    into the tangled heartland
where there is no trail, blue
                    hole in a cold blue sky.
Under a flat stone, you find
    a note you once wrote to yourself.
It says, The trouble with love.

BRAHMS SEXTET IN B-FLAT MAJOR

Take me to a place of murmuring water
                & I will nourish your weary soul,
says Johannes Brahms. Take me out
                    to breakfast, says my daughter
Elena, for I'm romantically involved
                  with blueberry waffles. The cello
throbs a mournful *sostenuto*, one note
                strung like rope across a canyon
of time to an old man alone with books,
   a box of photos. It could be me, searching
for erotic meaning in the word *sextet*.

In profile, straw-colored hair
                falling like arpeggios, Elena
is as beautiful as any bird I've seen,
                including the cormorant. Violins
talk fervidly about yellow leaves, autumn.
           Music rises, then subsides as if a fierce
warrior, fallen in battle, yearning
                for heaven, has stopped to kiss
his children. I think of zealot martyrs
      wired for devastation, their paradise

of virgins. Endless grief. My paradise
                is a cabin in the woods, a quiet stream,
Latin dance with Kristen, my friend
                whose hips in polyrhythm dispute
accepted laws of physics. You get happy
                when you drink wine,
says Elena. It's music,
   I say, how it restores the silence
where she grew up

& so did I. All that time.
                I had cross words with her
only once. She cried. I felt sick at heart,

                    because she lost the wingnut
to my Boy Scout mess kit
                    which I cherished
because of the word *boy*. Because
          I built a fire & fried rainbow trout
& was once a boy, this Brahms
                    sextet stirs my soul. Brahms
had something to say, couldn't
          say it in words & if he could
it would be this—

The domed chandelier on the ceiling
          is shaped like a woman's breast.
Mother's milk is what we mean
                    when we say *love*. Light
is crystalline. All of us are lost
          in dark space searching
for the EXIT sign in red,
                    then the big ending.

The world would be different
                    says Elena, if Brahms
knew Latin rhythms. Only one
          glass of chardonnay & I say
I don't need wine to be happy
                    when I'm with you.

RIVER UNDER ICE

April morning. Light
leaps through a window.
        What happens
in the mind's eye
        happens—you & I,
            specks of dust
jitterbugging in a sunbeam
                    toward each other.

        *

We're seeds a blackbird
            dropped in a meadow.
To soak in the sun & rain
        of each other, to flower
untamed, to heal a wound
                that never closes.

February. The river is moving
        under the ice.

        *

We'll remember July, hillside
by the old school, swath
                of tailfeathers fallen
from a small brown bird
                I held in my hand
    for you to see it breathing.

Publication Credits

The author gratefully acknowledges the time, energy and devotion to poetry, often voluntary, of the editors and staff where many of these poems first appeared, including the chapbooks *Rooster* (Main Street Rag, 2004), *How Many Faces Do You Have?* (Texas Review Press, 2016) and *Elvis Night at Johnny's* (Broadstone Books, 2022), along with these journals and anthologies:

Notre Dame Review, "Dark Matter," "Once Upon a Time"
Atlanta Review, "Guayaba," "Love Me Like the First Word"
Sycamore Review, "The Car Window"
slipstream, "Monologue for Long Afternoons"
HEArt, "Nightfall Near Matagalpa," "Photograph in *TIME*, 1985"
Antietam Review, "Rooster"
The 2001 Emily Dickinson Award Anthology, "The Way Your Fingers"
Pittsburgh Post-Gazette, "Spring Mills for Christmas"
An Eye for an Eye Makes the Whole World Blind: Poets on 9/11, "Salem Hill Hymn Sing"
Poetry, "The Painter Francis Bacon Plays Mountain Music"
Poet Lore, "Spring Mills"
Paper Street, "Managua Afternoon"
Main Street Rag, "Ode to Lonely Guys," "Ya No Puede," "Hound Dog Blues"
Passager, "Breath Through Bones"
5 AM, "Flower Man"
The Fourth River, "Crows," "How Well I Go with Sand & Gravel"
Fission of Form, Pittsburgh Society of Sculptors, "Untitled Copper and Steel"
Hunger Mountain, "August Night"
Motif Vol. 2: Come What May, "Rainy November Again"
Motif Vol. 3: All The Livelong Day, "Western Medicine"
Cimarron Review, "Buenos Aires"
U.S. 1 Worksheets, "The Trouble with Love," "River Under Ice"
Chautauqua, "Country of Silence"
The Florida Review, "Skin," "Flight to Yucatan," "Sleeplessness"
New Ohio Review, "Fastball Shy"
Tar River Poetry, "Beach Below the House at Plymouth"
The Comstock Review, "I Want You"
The Boom Project: Voices of a Generation, "Old Blue Volvo"
Poets Meet Politics 2022 Hungry Hill Anthology, "Without Moons or Lilies"

Thanks also to Michael Simms for the online journal *Vox Populi*, where some of these poems have been re-published.

Acknowledgments

My gratitude to family—including grandparents, parents, my daughter Elena, Kevin, William & Catherine, Lorraine Higgins—and to many fellow poets runs deeper than I can express. Near top-of-mind are the Pittsburgh group of writers, East End Poets, including Arlene Weiner, whose literate comments are a model for group process. Especially high on the list of poets whose work has pushed me toward finding my own best words & ways to arrange them are the late Tony Hoagland and Dean Young. I've learned from their teaching and prose as well as their poetry.

Among poet friends and correspondents, I've much appreciated (and my work benefitted from) knowing Beth Gylys. Likewise, I can't say enough about former Kentucky poet-laureate, Jeff Worley—with warm regard for his work and patient guidance of mine.

Thanks also to the Vermont Studio Center for opportunities to retreat from full-time work into the company of artists. Thanks to Larry Moore of Broadstone Books—a pleasure to have published with him. For helpful advice in structuring this book, thanks to TJ Beitelman. For literary friendship, I cherish many conversations with Professor Robert Gale (1919–2020). For friendship nourished in the joyfulness of music, I hold deep affection for Jan Hamilton.

About the Author

JAN HAMILTON

Mike Schneider began writing during the Vietnam War when, while serving at an air force base in Ohio, he published an anti-war "underground" newspaper. He has practiced law, worked as a science writer, won awards for magazine writing, and written book reviews and essays on culture for several publications. For a series of essays on art and politics in the Thomas Merton Center's *New People,* he received a 2003–04 Creative Artists Stipend in Arts Commentary from the Pennsylvania Council on the Arts. Three times nominated for the Pushcart Prize, his poems appear in many literary journals, several anthologies and three chapbooks. He received the 2012 Editors' Award from *The Florida Review* and the 2016 Robert Phillips Prize from Texas Review Press. With a colleague in 2010, he founded East End Poets, a group of Pittsburgh-based writers who meet to share their work. In 2017, for the Lifelong Learning program at Carnegie Mellon University, he taught the first course on Bob Dylan in Pittsburgh. Recently, the Hungry Hill Writing Group in West Cork, Ireland, awarded Schneider's work second prize in its *Poets Meet Politics 2022* International Open. He lives in Pittsburgh's historic South Side neighborhood.

www.ingramcontent.com/pod-product-compliance
Lightning Source LLC
Chambersburg PA
CBHW020215090426
42734CB00008B/1086